Summary and Analysis of

THINKING, FAST AND SLOW

Based on the Book
by Daniel Kahneman

WORTH BOOKS
SMART SUMMARIES

This Worth Books book is based on the 2013 paperback edition of *Thinking, Fast and Slow* by Daniel Kahneman published by Farrar, Straus and Giroux.

Summary and analysis copyright © 2017 by Open Road Integrated Media, Inc.

ISBN: 978-1-5040-4675-6

Worth Books
180 Maiden Lane
Suite 8A
New York, NY 10038
www.worthbooks.com

WORTH BOOKS
SMART SUMMARIES

Worth Books is a division of Open Road Integrated Media, Inc.

Contents

Context

Originally published in 2011, *Thinking, Fast and Slow* encapsulates approximately thirty years of psychologist Daniel Kahneman's work in behavioral economics and social and cognitive psychology. In the early 1970s, Kahneman and his research partner, Amos Tversky, began working to expose cognitive biases inherent to the human mind, particularly in the context of economic choices.

In 2002, Kahneman won the Nobel Prize in Economic Sciences for the work that became this book (Tversky died in 1996), which is especially notable because Kahneman is not an economist. *Thinking, Fast and Slow* is, in part, a long-form explanation of his Nobel Prize–winning work, geared toward laypeople and experts alike. The book also includes the author's work on judgment heuristics, which expands upon concepts discussed in Kahneman and Tversky's groundbreaking "Judgment Under Uncertainty: Heuristics and Biases," originally published in the journal *Science* in 1974.

With awareness of the two kinds of thinking we do—fast and slow—readers will learn how to better understand their own decision making and the choices made by others.

Overview

In this book, readers learn how both the automatic and the more rational thought processes of the brain work. We see that our natural human reason actually causes us to engage in various fallacies and systematic errors. Therefore, in order to make better decisions and formulate superior solutions to problems—as individuals, as businesses, and as societies—we must be able to identify and understand these biases, and learn to deal with them.

Summary

Part 1: Two Systems

System 1 of your brain operates speedily and automatically, while System 2 is slow and requires a great deal of mental energy to process complex mental activities. System 1 and System 2 work together.

Here are some examples of automatic activities attributed to System 1:

- Detect if one object is more distant than another
- Complete simple math equations, like $1 + 1 = ?$
- Smile when shown an image of puppies

- Complete the phrase, "salt and . . ."
- Orient to the source of a sound
- Swat a mosquito
- Drive on an empty road
- Recognize stereotypes

All of these mental calculations occur automatically and require very little or no effort. System 1 also includes innate skills, or those we share with other animals, such as being prepared to perceive the world, avoiding losses, recognizing objects, and fearing spiders. Many more we acquire through practice and learned associations and abilities, such as knowing the capital of New York, reading, and interpreting social situations. Additionally, many of the mental actions attributed to System 1 are involuntary. Your mind cannot help but solve 1 + 1.

Here are some examples of the mental events attributed to System 2:

- Focus on the voice of one person in a noisy room
- Look for a woman with red hair in a crowd
- Focus your attention on only the elephants in a circus
- Maintain a faster walking speed than is comfortable for you
- Fill out a tax form

- Search your memory for a surprising sound
- Brace for a punch
- Monitor how you act in a social situation

Unlike the mental events attributed to System 1, System 2 events require you to pay attention. Paying attention requires you to spend mental energy. Usually, you can only process one System 2 mental event at a time. For example, it is impossible for most people to make a left turn in heavy traffic while calculating 19 x 168. Focusing intently on something effectively makes you blind, even to stimuli that normally attract attention.

System 1:

System 1 responses are immediate, which means they can easily be erroneous and are often based on inadequate information; they are essential to human survival, however, because they make instant judgments in potentially dangerous situations. For example, System 1 tells you to move from the path of an oncoming cyclist, swat a mosquito, or duck to avoid a projectile.

System 1's main job is to assess normality, the evolutionary function that helps us survive—life is more manageable when there are patterns to follow. It seeks out causes and intentions, and can attribute effects to them even when there is no actual causality. The "halo effect," for instance, occurs when the brain uses a small amount of information to form broad, sweeping conclusions about someone or something without considering what information might be missing.

This system pulls from the many ideas we unconsciously group together at any given time to instantly make sense of situations and stimuli around us. Priming effects are an expression of this. When your brain has been primed by exposure to an idea, theme, or even by your own physiological needs, you more readily pull related associations from your existing networks. Primes guide our behaviors, making us more or less likely to act in certain ways. For example, research shows that voters from both ends of the political spectrum are more likely to vote to increase school budgets when their polling place is inside a school. This is a priming effect.

System 2:

System 2 involves exerting a high level of effort, which causes the brain to "not see" other stimuli, even when those stimuli would normally be remarkable. In fact, tasks handled by this second system result in physical changes to our bodies: pupil dilation and increased heart rate—the two signs Kahneman used to research how and when people switched back and forth between the mental processes.

This system operates at a slower speed. Pushing it to work much faster takes considerable effort and depletes the brain's resources quickly. The mind is cognitively busy when it is intensely focused on tasks that demand System 2's energies, such as calculating numbers. But being cognitively busy also renders one more likely to make superficial judgments and impulsive decisions. This is because System 2, the home of good judgment, is occupied, so System 1 is forced to take over.

Real cognitive aptitude is the heart of System 2, and it's what gives us the ability to think and consider our options before acting, to employ self-control, and to come to rational decisions.

Clashes Between System 1 and System 2:

System 1 monitors what is going on around us by constantly engaging in basic assessments; it believes and confirms what it sees, while System 2 doubts and challenges. System 1 is unable to focus only on the task assigned to it by System 2; inevitably, it performs other basic assessments as well.

When an intuitive answer to a question isn't readily available, System 1 generates an easier question, substitutes it, and answers it. Kahneman defines this as a heuristic: a simple process to find answers to hard questions, even though those answers may not be perfect. Issues arise when the heuristics generated are inadequate substitutes. The mood heuristic is the way the mind substitutes an assessment of a current mood for the more complicated question of general happiness or other emotional assessment. The affect heuristic refers to the way we tend to allow our likes and dislikes to control our beliefs about the world.

Cognitive ease is the feeling you have when things are generally going well and there is no need for System 2 to intervene. Cognitive strain is the feeling that there are unmet needs that require work from System 2. Mere familiarity can be enough to trick the brain into thinking something is true. Things that are easier to read and understand feel truer to us. Things that are tougher to read and understand induce cognitive strain and therefore engage System 2.

Mood affects intuition, because good mood and cognitive ease go together. Bad mood and cognitive strain are associated because tougher times demand System 2. When you are feeling happy you may be more creative, but you may also be more prone to logical errors.

Need to Know: System 1 works automatically and looks for patterns around you; it makes snap judgments, which may be erroneous if the problem at hand is complex. System 2 doubts and challenges, but is lazy. Sometimes the latter should take over, but instead it relies on what the former tells it.

Part 2: Heuristics and Biases

Humans are not intuitively good at statistics; in fact, System 1 finds relationships and causality where none exist, leading to a bias of confidence over doubt. This is a problem even for trained experts who understand statistics, because System 1 works automatically.

The Anchoring Effect:

The anchoring effect occurs when people consider some value for an unknown number before estimating that number. Even when the considered value is completely random and unrelated, subsequent estimates tend to be "anchored" to it. For example, if you are hoping to buy a car that is listed at $40,000 and then get 10 percent off, you feel you've gotten a deal in paying $36,000. However, that may be because you've "anchored" to that initial $40,000. In fact, $40,000 may be totally irrelevant to the car's actual value.

Availability:

The availability heuristic means that our estimate of how prevalent something is or how frequently it happens is heavily influenced by how easily we can call up examples of the phenomenon and how recently we were exposed to it. For instance, if in your recent memory several famous musicians died young, you may be inclined to think that the majority of musicians die young.

Availability causes a bias in how we assess risk. Trends in reporting cause people to "see" more about some kinds of risk than others, and therefore attach more importance to them. In reality, one type of risk may be far less significant than another. Because its job is to sense danger, it is System 1 that responds to these kinds of trends. But thanks to the availability bias, actions can result in inappropriate or ineffective responses.

Representativeness:

Humans tend to predict probability based on representativeness rather than base rates. This happens when System 1 substitutes simple-to-answer heuristic questions in place of actual base-rate calculations of probability—we guess how likely things are to happen based on intuitive judgments. Instead, we should anchor our estimates to reliable diagnostic evidence and base rates.

Statistical base rates characterize the populations involved in a case, but not the facts of the specific case itself. As we try to form judgments and predictions, we tend to undervalue statistical base rates and overvalue causal base rates—even though they have the same relevance as each other. The stereotypes of System 1 shape this process; Bayesian analysis is a statistical tool that can mitigate these effects because it works with base rates and removes intuition from the process. The theorem is an algorithm that allows the user to plug in the known data and base rates and arrive at a logical prediction.

The Linda Problem:

Another common System 1 error is mistaking plausibility for probability. Kahneman illustrates this by detailing a well-known experiment he and his partner conducted. It is called the Linda problem: Linda is a social activist. Is she more likely to be a bank teller or a feminist bank teller? Obviously she's statistically more likely to be a bank teller, because all feminist bank tellers are bank tellers. If we choose "feminist bank teller" as the answer, we are limiting our own odds of being right. Many people get this answer wrong, however, because this scenario fools System 1. The job of System 1 is simply to assess plausibility, and feminist bank teller "feels" more plausible to System 1.

Regression to the Mean:

Random fluctuations in the quality of human performance mean that particularly bad or good outcomes are more likely to be followed by less spectacular outcomes in the other direction. This is called regression to the mean. For example, if a fighter pilot in a training program has a particularly bad flight, he or she is highly likely to have a better flight the next time, no matter whether praise or punishment follows that bad flight.

Most psychologists have found that praise is more effective in training overall as time passes, but many military trainers believe that criticism and punishment are more effective. Why? Because they see a very bad flight, followed immediately by punishment, followed by a better flight. They assume that there is a cause and effect in action. However, statistically speaking, the better flight was highly likely to occur anyway; the bad flight was simply a regression to the mean.

Need to Know: A trait of System 1 is a willingness to base extreme and rare predictions on weak evidence. System 1 will often substitute heuristic, or easier, questions and answers into contexts that are too complex, thereby avoiding analysis and data-driven decisions.

Part 3: Overconfidence

Our expectations for the future are strongly shaped by the stories we tell about the past; unfortunately, the brain retells incomplete versions that are based on hindsight. This narrative fallacy leads to outcome bias: the mistaken idea that a poor decision that happened to turn out well was actually a good decision. These are called cognitive illusions. For example, investors and pundits believe that they have the skill and talent to make successful predictions, even though there is no concrete data to support that contention. In fact, the numbers indicate that most success in these areas is based on luck.

Algorithms are significantly more accurate in predicting outcomes than intuition is, even the intuitions of experts. The same experts, given the exact same case materials in different settings, contradict their own evaluations about 20% of the time. This is because System 1 is dependent on context.

For true expertise to develop without the illusion of validity, there must be two conditions present: a predictable environment and the chance to learn about the factors that make the environment predictable. In other words, enough practice and exposure can allow a level of expertise that makes even complicated assessments automatic. For example, a chess master can glance at a board and instantly "know" the right moves and the outcome of the game, while for most people, that series of calculations would demand the employment of System 2.

The planning fallacy describes predictions that are unrealistic best-case scenarios which could be made more accurate by using reference-case forecasting—a way of anchoring predictions to statistics surrounding similar cases. The sunk-cost fallacy is a related issue in which a plan that should be abandoned is pursued because no one wants to admit defeat. While the believed reason for pursuing the plan may be unwillingness to lose money already invested, careful analysis of the plan and its probable outcome can reveal the high likelihood of losing more money, which shows the reasoning to be faulty.

Entrepreneurial delusions are a kind of optimism in which business owners do not realistically assess their chances of success. They also have an illusion of being in control of the entire situation and therefore cognitively neglect the impact of competitors.

Need to Know: Look for ways to adopt algorithms in decision making to improve your outcomes. This may mean learning to use Bayes's theorem when making predictions, for example, or learning to anchor your assessments to realistic base rates and other data sources, rather than unrelated anchors or intuitions.

Part 4: Choices

The choices dealt with in this section have to do with wealth, risk, and loss. Kahneman is concerned with how System 1 and System 2 affect our perception of risks, losses, and how we accumulate (and lose) wealth.

Utility Theory:

According to Bernoulli's utility theory, risk-averse people choose a sure thing that is lesser in value, essentially paying to avoid uncertainty. Bernoulli's model states that it is the utility of wealth—not the money itself, but what can be done with money—that makes people happy. However, Kahneman argues that this ignores reference points; a person who is faced only with bad outcomes is more likely to take a risk, even when the practical numerical outcome is the same as the one faced by the risk-averse person.

In other words, if utility theory is true, and you and I each have one million dollars, we should both be equally happy because we have the same ability to accomplish things with the same amount of wealth. However, this ignores our individual reference points. If you had ten million dollars yesterday and I had one thousand, chances are you are far less happy than I am now.

Prospect Theory:

In contrast to utility theory, prospect theory is shaped by three cognitive features: evaluation is relative to a neutral reference point, there is diminishing sensitivity to changes in wealth, and we all share an aversion to loss. It also considers the endowment effect—the feeling that something is worth more once you already have it, which is itself based on a reference point.

For Kahneman, the most important takeaways from prospect theory are that reference points exist, and losses always loom larger than corresponding gains in our perception. Therefore, because existing terms provide reference points for negotiations, people tend to fight harder to prevent losses than they do to achieve gains, and they have a sense of unfairness or entitlement which pushes them to feel that their losses are unjust.

The Fourfold Pattern:

Kahneman and Tversky came up with a way to explain a system of preferences called the fourfold pattern. Two main ideas are at the heart of this: 1.) people attach values not to wealth, but to losses and gains, and 2.) people attach decision weights to outcomes that differ from actual probabilities. These patterns give rise to four scenarios:

- When facing a gain with a low probability, the possibility effect—mistaking something that is merely possible for something that is probable—induces risk-seeking behavior: We buy a lottery ticket even though it is a waste of money.
- When facing a loss with a low probability, the possibility effect induces risk-averse behavior: We pay for insurance so we don't lose everything in a fire.
- When facing a gain with a high probability, the certainty effect induces risk-averse behavior: We take a "sure thing," $80 today, instead of a highly "likely" $100 tomorrow.
- When facing a loss with a high probability, the certainty effect induces risk-seeking behavior: We go ahead and gamble instead of cutting our losses.

Rare Events:

In the decision-making process, people overweigh and overestimate the probability of unlikely events. Vivid events, obsessive concerns, explicit reminders, and concrete representations are given more importance and are seen as more probable. For example, most people in the United States today fear a terrorist act more than a car accident or a heart attack, even though statistically they have far more risk from the latter two possible events. However, terror attacks are vivid events and we see explicit reminders of them in the media every day; therefore, we give them more importance as we decide what is probable.

Making Decisions:

It is more useful to develop a risk policy that can be routinely applied than to face each risky choice individually. A risk policy embeds a single risky choice in the context of similar choices and avoids optimism bias and overly narrow framing, which can lead to choices that are too risk-averse. A risk policy is a way to avoid narrow framing and apply reasonable approaches to risks across the board instead of on a case-by-case basis.

For example, someone who takes the daily fluctuations of the stock market too seriously is likely to be a poor investor. Every loss or gain will be felt too closely by that person; only larger patterns should induce decision making. A risk policy in this context might be to simply evaluate one's portfolio only once every quarter. This can help avoid poor decisions based on smaller, daily changes rather than larger, overall trends.

Another example might be deciding whether or not to buy an extended warranty. If you just had a bad

experience with an electronic device, you might be will-
ing to pay a high premium for an extended warranty.
However, statistically, the odds that you'll need one
again could be very low; perhaps you've never needed
a warranty before in your entire buying history. The
risk policy in this case would probably be to not buy
extended warranties. In this example, the risk policy
would be saving you from making the emotional decision to buy the warranty right after a bad experience.

Rational decision making is, by definition, concerned only with future consequences of current
decisions, and has no stake in justifying past decisions. However, humans tend to base their decisions, in whole or in part, on positions that validate
past actions. They also avoid decisions and risks that
might induce regret.

Rationality tends to be better served by more com-
prehensive, broader frames, such as joint evaluation
in context rather than single evaluation. For example,
as you set out to buy a new air conditioning unit, you
may see that the unit you're looking at carries a certain BTU capacity. This may not mean much to you in
isolation, but if you engage in a joint evaluation of the
BTUs of different models, you'll see that units vary
widely based on BTUs and that this metric is related
to how much power the unit has and how much it
costs to run. You may not need a high-BTU air condi-
tioner to cool off a small room.

Without basis for comparison, you are more likely to produce an emotional System 1 decision. Proper framing of questions is conducive to rational decision making because it allows you to see the full picture as you decide what you'll do. After a very bad day, you're likely to make emotional decisions based on that experience. However, if you can hold off and place the experience in the larger context of your life overall, your decisions will be more rational and less emotional.

Need to Know: Apply risk policies routinely to embed each risky choice in the context of similar choices and avoid optimism bias, overly narrow framing, and adjustment of current decisions for past behaviors. Use broad frames such as joint evaluation to create risk policies for rational decision making.

Part 5: Two Selves

The formulation of memories is based largely on primacy, recency, intensity, and frequency. Therefore, if a person was married for twenty years and the last two were horrible, he or she may say that it was a terrible marriage, even if most of it wasn't. This is an example of duration neglect, which can affect rational decision making.

Focusing illusions and affective forecasting cause errors in judgment. For example, we often pin our happiness on the attainment of material objects, only to feel disappointed when we get those objects and happiness still eludes us. We also erroneously link memories to our current moods: For example, if you are having an especially bad day and someone asks about your job satisfaction or marriage, you're more likely to give negative assessments than you would on a better day. By linking mood and memory, we misinterpret our own needs and wants, and therefore take actions which are less than optimal.

Humans are not inherently irrational, but we need more help in making better decisions and forming accurate judgments. We also need tools to cope with those who would exploit the weaknesses of System 1 and System 2 and the ways they interact. For example, some advertisers relish and count on our poor decision-making abilities, seeking to take advantage of our moments of snap emotional decision making. We can cope with these people and the cognitive traps they lay for us by generally working to make more rational decisions as a matter of course.

Need to Know: We can avoid System 1 errors by recognizing when we are in dangerous waters, cognitively speaking, slowing our process down, and engaging System 2 for help.

Timeline

1969: Daniel Kahneman and Amos Tversky meet at the Hebrew University of Jerusalem. Their meeting inspires their work together, which lasts more or less until Tversky dies in 1996.

1974: The two psychologists publish "Judgment Under Uncertainty: Heuristics and Biases," in *Science*. The research was supported by the Department of Defense. By the time *Thinking, Fast and Slow* was written, it was one of the most highly cited articles in social science and remains so today.

1979: Kahneman and Tversky publish "Prospect Theory: An Analysis of Decision under Risk," in

Econometrica, which provided the basis for the study of behavioral economics.

1983: The duo presents "Choices, Values, and Frames," at a meeting of the American Psychological Association. This work is published in print form in *American Psychologist* in 1984.

1996: Amos Tversky dies of cancer.

2002: Daniel Kahneman receives the Nobel Prize in Economics. The committee primarily cites the 1974 and 1984 works.

2011: Kahneman publishes *Thinking, Fast and Slow*, which receives numerous accolades.

Direct Quotes and Analysis

"The gorilla study illustrates two important facts about our minds: we can be blind to the obvious, and we are also blind to our blindness."

In the experiment referred to above, a number of people are shown a short video of basketball players on a court and are assigned a very specific task: to count the number of passes made by the players in white shorts. The level of focus required here is high, and it prevents about half of all respondents from seeing a woman in a gorilla suit who enters the court and remains there for about nine full seconds. Had participants not been counting passes, it is unlikely any of them would have missed the obvious discontinuity.

"Whether professionals have a chance to develop intuitive expertise depends essentially on the quality and speed of feedback, as well as on sufficient opportunity to practice."

In other words, it is possible for a true expert to have an automatic, System 1-style intuition that includes real expertise, but only under certain conditions. Useful intuition is only based on expertise when enough learning has taken place to make the process automatic; a fast feedback loop can improve upon an expert's ability to internalize and act upon his or her learning (anesthesiologists can see the effects of their work with a patient immediately, whereas radiologists do not receive immediate review of the accuracy of their diagnoses).

"The people who have the greatest influence on the lives of others are likely to be optimistic and overconfident, and to take more risks than they realize."

Optimistic bias plays a critical role in progress because risk taking is frightening, and most of us are risk averse to some extent. Optimistic actors are confident, and they are better able to secure assistance from others as they pursue their endeavors, which helps to improve their chances.

"Although Humans are not irrational, they often need help to make more accurate judgments and better decisions, and in some cases policies and institutions can provide that help."

This cuts against the idea that the rational person should be entirely free, and in no need of guidance. The traditional related public policy ideal is to avoid restricting individual rights to choose unless those choices cause harm to others. In contrast, Kahneman's position, based on behavioral economics, includes a sense of choice architecture. This concept suggests that societies have some obligation to properly frame the choices to be made by individuals to promote better outcomes for the group as well as the individual.

"You may not know that you are optimistic about a project because something about its leader reminds you of your sister, or that you dislike a person who looks vaguely like your dentist. If asked for an explanation, however, you will search your memory for presentable reasons and will certainly find some. Moreover, you will believe the story you make up."

System 1 intrudes upon our decision-making process all the time, whether or not we are aware of it. Remember that System 1 is the "thinking fast" that we do.

This problem is most likely to come into play during cognitively challenging times. The advice Kahneman offers is that we take the time to do some "thinking slow" and apply our rational focus when the need to make critical decisions arises.

Trivia

1. Daniel Kahneman cited his experiences in Nazi Germany as a force which shaped his lifelong interest in human psychology. One evening in 1942, as he walked home past curfew with his sweater inside out to hide the Jewish star he was forced to wear, he encountered an SS soldier. Terrified, he tried to hurry past, only to be shocked by what the soldier did:

"He beckoned me over, picked me up, and hugged me. I was terrified that he would notice the star inside my sweater. He was speaking to me with great emotion, in German. When he put me down, he opened his wallet, showed me a picture of a boy, and gave me some money. I went home more certain than ever that my mother was right: people were endlessly complicated and interesting."

2. The classic 1974 study "Judgment Under Uncertainty: Heuristics and Biases," which led to *Thinking, Fast and Slow*, was supported by the Department of Defense. This was a natural culmination of Kahneman's military work experience: in 1955, he joined the Psychology branch of the Israel Defense Forces, where he assessed candidates for officer training. It was this work which provided the seed for his discovery of "the illusion of validity."

3. Kahneman's PhD dissertation was somewhat less of a masterpiece than his other work. Completed over the course of eight days in 1961, Kahneman commented about the paper, "That was probably the last time I wrote anything without pain." His teacher, Susan Ervin, described her experience reading the dissertation as "wading through wet mush."

4. Kahneman credits Amos Tversky with giving much of the direction and force to their joint work and writing. He also cites Tversky's sense of

humor as a critical factor in their collaboration, remarking, "I have probably shared more than half of the laughs of my life with Amos."

5. Tversky and Kahneman's theories have not always been well received. In fact, they've occasionally attracted serious criticism, especially in the 1970s. For this reason, Kahneman admits to a deep level of personal discomfort with professional anger, and says that as a result he will not referee any papers that might make him feel angry. This is, in a very real sense, a workaround for his own System 1 biases.

6. In 2016, bestselling author Michael Lewis published a book on the collaboration between Daniel Kahneman and Amos Tversky, *The Undoing Project: A Friendship That Changed Our Minds.*

7. Daniel Kahneman and Amos Tversky have been called "the Lennon and McCartney of behavioural psychology" by Tim Adams, a staff writer for the *Guardian.*

What's That Word?

3-D heuristic: A cognitive bias or illusion in which the perception of an object seen in two dimensions that you understand to be a three-dimensional object can be swayed by your notions of depth and distance.

Add-1 task: An exercise to fully engage System 2 in which you add digits in time to a rhythmic beat.

Affect heuristic: The concept of decisions that are guided by one's likes and dislikes, rather than reasoning or deliberation.

Anchoring: A cognitive bias that describes the tendency to rely too much on an initial piece of random information—the anchor—which is then used to make subsequent decisions.

Availability cascade: A self-sustaining chain of events growing from a minor event into large-scale panic that is fed as emotional reactions continue the cycle and increased availability of the information makes the risk seem more severe.

Base rate: Commonly used in statistics, a base rate is the proportion of a test group that has a particular property. To calculate the likelihood of picking a red marble out of an urn, for example, one needs to know how many marbles there are in the urn and how many of them are red.

Basic assessments: The countless estimates System 1 conducts automatically to ensure the personal safety of the individual in his or her surroundings.

Bayesian analysis: A method using Bayes's theorem to update a prediction or probability as more information or evidence becomes available. In the context of this work, it is a way to counteract System 1 errors.

Behavioral economics: A school of thought that analyzes human behavior through applied psychological insight in order to explain economic decision making.

Certainty effect: The psychological effect which causes us to underestimate and underappreciate the probability of outcomes that are almost certain (from 95% to 100%).

Cognitive busyness: The state of having System 2 occupied with cognitive tasks.

Cognitive ease: The feeling that things are going well, no threats are present, and there is otherwise no need to engage System 2.

Cognitive illusions: Illusions of thought.

Cognitive strain: A mental state resulting from an exertion of cognitive effort combined with the presence of unmet demands, which leads to discomfort and more demands on System 2.

Confirmation bias: The tendency to interpret new evidence to confirm existing theories or beliefs.

Conjunction fallacy: The formal logical fallacy of believing that specific conditions are more probable than a single, more general condition (As illustrated in the Linda problem, it is often presumed that Linda is more likely to be a feminist bank teller than a bank teller).

Duration neglect: The tendency of people to mostly neglect duration in their judgments of the unpleasantness of painful experiences.

Ego depletion: The idea that we can only control or will a limited amount of mental resources, and that when the reserve of energy for mental activity is low, self-control is impaired. These conditions together make up a state of ego depletion.

Endowment effect: The theory that people value things more when they own them.

Focusing illusion: The tendency to exaggerate the importance of one part of an event or idea.

Framing: A cognitive bias in which we make choices based on whether they are presented as gains or losses.

Halo effect: A cognitive bias in which a person's general feelings or impressions of something influence his or her ideas about every aspect of that thing.

Heuristic: A simple procedure that helps find adequate, albeit imperfect, answers to difficult questions.

Hindsight bias: The tendency to overestimate one's ability to have predicted an outcome, although such prediction was impossible.

Intensity matching: The ability to move back and forth between variables intuitively.

Law of small numbers: A cognitive bias that happens when people assume that they can estimate the characteristics of a sample population from a small number of data points or observations.

Loss aversion: The strong preference most people tend to have for avoiding losses over acquiring gains.

Mental shotgun: The process inside our brains whereby we intend to compute something specific but produce more information than we need without trying.

Mere exposure effect: The tendency to prefer things merely because they are familiar.

Narrative fallacy: The limited ability humans have to view facts without weaving a uniting story or series of linking relationships into them.

Optimistic bias: The tendency to underestimate the likelihood of experiencing adverse events.

Outcome bias: A cognitive bias in which decisions are judged by their outcomes rather than the quality of the actual decisions at the time they were made.

Planning fallacy: The tendency to display optimism bias in estimating how much time a future task will require.

Priming: An implicit memory effect in which exposure to one thing influences the way we respond to another.

Prospect theory: The theory of behavioral economics that describes how people choose between risky probabilistic alternatives when they know the probabilities of outcomes.

Regression to the mean: The statistical phenomenon of extreme values being followed by values that are closer to the average.

Risk aversion: Human behavior in the face of uncertainty that seeks to reduce that uncertainty.

Sunk-cost fallacy: The tendency to continue with an undertaking if you have already invested a substantial amount of effort, time, or money, even when continuing is not the most prudent option.

System 1: Thought process that is automatic, emotional, instinctive, and biased to believe.

System 2: Thought process that is deliberate, logical, slower, and more likely to doubt or question.

Theory-induced blindness: Once a theory is accepted, it is very difficult to notice its flaws.

What you see is all there is (WYSIATI): The tendency to use the information at hand as if it is the only information.

Critical Response

- A 2011 *Los Angeles Times* Book Prize winner
- A *Globe and Mail* Best Book of the Year, 2011
- A *New York Times* bestseller
- A *New York Times Book Review* Best Book of 2011
- An *Economist* Book of the Year, 2011
- A *Wall Street Journal* Best Nonfiction Book of the Year, 2011
- A National Academy of Sciences Best Book Award winner, 2012

"A sweeping, compelling tale of just how easily our brains are bamboozled, bringing in both his own research and that of numerous psychologists, econo-

mists, and other experts.... Kahneman has a remarkable ability to take decades worth of research and distill from it what would be important and interesting for a lay audience."   —Jesse Singal,
                                        The Boston Globe

"It is an astonishingly rich book: lucid, profound, full of intellectual surprises and self-help value. . . . So impressive is its vision of flawed human reason that the *New York Times* columnist David Brooks recently declared that Kahneman and Tversky's work 'will be remembered hundreds of years from now,' and that it is 'a crucial pivot point in the way we see ourselves.'"
                    —*The New York Times Book Review*

"Profound . . . As Copernicus removed the Earth from the centre of the universe and Darwin knocked humans off their biological perch, Mr. Kahneman has shown that we are not the paragons of reason we assume ourselves to be."   —*The Economist*

"An outstandingly clear and precise study of the 'dual-process' model of the brain and our embedded self-delusions."   —*The Guardian*

"It is impossible to exaggerate the importance of Daniel Kahneman's contribution to the understanding of the way we think and choose. He stands among the giants, a weaver of the threads of Charles Darwin, Adam Smith and Sigmund Freud. Arguably the most important psychologist in history, Kahneman has reshaped cognitive psychology, the analysis of rationality and reason, the understanding of risk and the study of happiness and well-being."

—*The Globe and Mail* (Toronto)

"Thanks to the elegance and force of his ideas, and the robustness of the evidence he offers for them, he has helped us to a new understanding of our divided minds—and our whole selves."

—*The Wall Street Journal*

"Synthesizing decades of his research, as well as that of colleagues, Kahneman lays out an architecture of human decision-making—a map of the mind that resembles a finely tuned machine with, alas, some notable trapdoors and faulty wiring."   —*Bloomberg*

About Daniel Kahneman

Daniel Kahneman is an Israeli-American psychologist and professor emeritus at the Woodrow Wilson School at Princeton University. He is best known for his work on the psychology of decision making and its impact on behavioral economics. His work challenges the idea—underpinning much of modern economic theory—that humans are essentially rational thinkers. With his research partner, Amos Tversky, and other experts, Kahneman established a cognitive basis for various frequently observed human errors and elucidated the biases and heuristics from which they arise.

He is an award-winning research scientist, scholar, psychologist, and lecturer. In 2002, his work won him the Nobel Prize in Economics. In 2011, he published his bestselling book, *Thinking, Fast and Slow*. In 2013, he received the Presidential Medal of Freedom in recognition of his work.

For Your Information

Online

"Dan's Interview with Nobelist Daniel Kahneman."
    DanPink.com
"Daniel Kahneman changed the way we think about
    thinking. But what do other thinkers think of
    him?" TheGuardian.com
"Daniel Kahneman: The Thought Leader Interview."
    Strategy-Business.com
"The King of Human Error." VanityFair.com
"The Quiz Daniel Kahneman Wants You to Fail."
    VanityFair.com
"Thinking, Fast and Slow." YouTube.com
"Two Brains Running." NYTimes.com

Books

The Better Angels of Our Nature by Steven Pinker

The (Honest) Truth about Dishonesty by Dan Ariely

The Improbability Principle: Why Coincidences, Miracles, and Rare Events Happen Every Day by David J. Hand

The Invisible Gorilla: How Our Intuitions Deceive Us by Christopher Chabris and Daniel Simons

Misbehaving: The Making of Behavioral Economics by Richard H. Thaler

On Being Certain by Robert Alan Burton

Sources of Power by Gary A. Klein

The Undoing Project: A Friendship That Changed Our Minds by Michael Lewis

Bibliography

Holt, Jim. "Two Brains Running," review of *Thinking, Fast and Slow*, by Daniel Kahneman. *New York Times*, November 25, 2011. http://www.nytimes .com/2011/11/27/books/review/thinking-fast-and-slow-by-daniel-kahneman-book-review.html.

Kahneman, Daniel. "Daniel Kahneman – Biographical." Nobelprize.org, accessed on December 23, 2016. http://www.nobelprize.org/nobel_prizes /economic-sciences/laureates/2002/kahneman-bio .html.

Kahneman, Daniel. "Daniel Kahneman: 'Thinking, Fast and Slow' | Talks at Google." Youtube, Nov ember 7, 2011. https://www.youtube.com/watch ?v=CjVQJdIrDJ0.

Kahneman, Daniel. *Thinking, Fast and Slow*. New York: Farrar, Straus and Giroux, 2011.

Lalinde, Jaime. "The Quiz Daniel Kahneman Wants You to Fail." *Vanity Fair*, November 4, 2011. http://www.vanityfair.com/news/2011/12/kahneman-quiz-201112.

Lewis, Michael. "The King of Human Error". *Vanity Fair, 2011*. http://www.vanityfair.com/news/2011/12/michael-lewis-201112.

Pinker, Steven, Richard Thaler, Richard Layard, Nassim Nicholas Taleb, and Sally Vickers. "Daniel Kahneman Changed the Way We Think about Thinking. But What Do Other Thinkers Think of Him?" *The Guardian*, February 16, 2014. https://www.theguardian.com/science/2014/feb/16/daniel-kahneman-thinking-fast-and-slow-tributes.

MORE SMART SUMMARIES
FROM WORTH BOOKS

BUSINESS

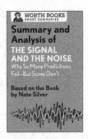

WORTH BOOKS
SMART SUMMARIES

MORE SMART SUMMARIES
FROM WORTH BOOKS

POPULAR SCIENCE

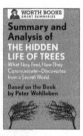

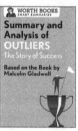

WORTH BOOKS
SMART SUMMARIES

INTEGRATED MEDIA

Find a full list of our authors and
titles at www.openroadmedia.com

FOLLOW US
@OpenRoadMedia